THE LITTLE BOOK OF

ULTIMATE DAD JOKES

Published in 2024 by OH!
An Imprint of Welbeck Non-Fiction Limited,
part of Welbeck Publishing Group.
Offices in: London – 20 Mortimer Street, London W1T 3JW
and Sydney – Level 17, 207 Kent St, Sydney NSW 2000 Australia
www.welbeckpublishing.com

ISBN 978-1-80069-622-8

Compiled and written by: Malcolm Croft
Editorial: Saneaah Muhammad
Project manager: Russell Porter
Production: Arlene Lestrade

A CIP catalogue record for this book is available from the British
Library

Printed in China

10 9 8 7 6 5 4 3 2 1

THE LITTLE BOOK OF
ULTIMATE
DAD JOKES

THE VERY BEST OF THE WORST

CONTENTS

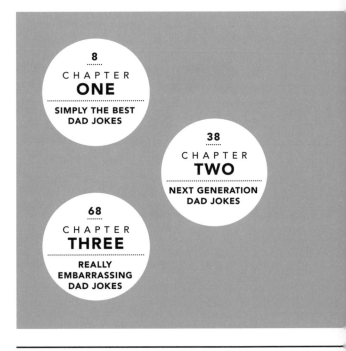

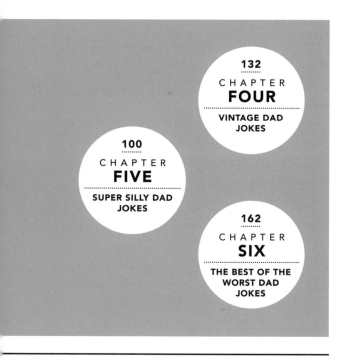

INTRODUCTION

Dear Dads,

Welcome to *The Little Book of Ultimate Dad Jokes* – Dad Jokes 2.0, if you will – the second serving of the super-selling original but better, badder and even more bonkers than before.

Why? You may plead… and beg… and yell. Because dads are worth it, that's why.

While this sequel may be terrible news – literally tearable – for mums, grandparents and children, decent upgrades like this are the stuff that make dads the happiest. A new treasure trove of comedy gold to plunder mercilessly; the perfect payback for all the times the kids refused to go to sleep.

For decades, doting fathers have loved nothing more than to dole out droll quips guaranteed to make his family's eyes roll quick. You see, a dad is powered – supercharged – by his family's disapproval, not beaten down by it. His family's groan and guffaws from his gags galore give dads a semblance of power in a household where he has increasingly little. A dad knows that one of his laser-guided jokes will clear any room in 0.5 seconds, giving him precisely the type of peace and quiet he deserves.

With more than 170 jokes, japes, jollies, jests and joshes (barely) restrained within this tiny tome, there is enough wholesome humour to make the entire family – including those cousins twice removed you never see – wish they'd never been born.

From humdinger puns to absurdly naff one-liners and all manner of silliness in-between this comprehensive compendium of comical calamity is a collection so cute and compact, dads all over the world now have no excuse to leave the front door without it.

Speaking of which…

Knock, knock.
Who's there?
Wooden shoe.
Wooden shoe who?

Wooden shoe like to hear another dad joke?

OK, and we're off… again!

....

CHAPTER
ONE

SIMPLY THE BEST DAD JOKES

"Remember: What dad really wants is a nap. Really."

Dave Barry

WHAT DO YOU CALL A FISH WEARING A BOWTIE?

Sofishticated

Why is swimming with sharks so expensive?

Because it costs an arm and a leg

DID YOU HEAR ABOUT THE GUY WHO DRANK INVISIBLE INK?

He's at the hospital waiting to be seen

Why did the computer catch a cold?

WHY DID THE BANANA GO TO THE DOCTOR?

Because it wasn't peeling well

What do you call a moose with no name?

Anonymoose

What do you get when you cross an elephant and a fish?

Swimming trunks

How do you get a mouse to smile?

Why did the whale blush?

It saw the ocean's bottom

Why are dads so good at napping?

Because they can do it with
their eyes closed!

I was going to tell a time-traveling dad joke, but you didn't like it.

What do you call a sleeping bull?

What did the banana say to the boy?

Nothing, bananas can't talk!

How do you open a banana?

What do you call a magician who's lost their magic?

Ian

Why didn't Han Solo enjoy his steak dinner?

What did Yoda say when he saw himself in 4K?

HDMI

WHAT DO YOU CALL A DINOSAUR THAT ASKS A LOT OF DEEP QUESTIONS?

Why do you never hear dad jokes about umbrellas?

They usually go over people's heads

What happens when it rains cats and dogs?

You have to be careful not to step in a poodle

WHY DO COWS WEAR BELLS?

Because their horns don't work

What's blue and doesn't weigh much?

WHAT DO YOU CALL A COW IN AN EARTHQUAKE?

A milkshake!

What do you call a werewolf who doesn't know they're a werewolf?

WHAT DO YOU GET WHEN YOU CROSS A MAN WITH THE HEART OF A LION?

A lifetime ban from the zoo

What do you call an Italian astronaut?

What kind of dinosaur has the biggest vocabulary?

The thesaurus!

What's a witch's favourite school subject?

CHAPTER
TWO

NEXT GENERATION DAD JOKES

"Dad taught me everything I know. Unfortunately, he didn't teach me everything he knows."

Al Unser

What did the dog say when it sat on sandpaper?

Ruff!

What does a triceratops sit on?

WHY DID THE CHICKEN CROSS THE PLAYGROUND?

To get to the other slide!

What's the difference between a rabbit and a plum?

Why don't dinosaurs talk?

Because they're dead!

What do you get when you mix a cocker spaniel, a poodle and a ghost?

WHAT'S THE SMELLIEST PLANET?

Poopiter

Two muffins were sitting in an oven. One turned to the other and said, "Wow, it's pretty hot in here."

The other one shouted, "Wow, a talking muffin!"

47

How do you get a hurt pig to a hospital in time?

In a hambulance

WHY DID THE COW JUMP OVER THE MOON?

What's E.T. short for?

Because he's only got tiny legs

What's orange and sounds like a parrot?

Have you heard the joke about retired people?

It doesn't work

What do dentists call their x-rays?

What happens when the future, the present and the past walk into a bar?

Things got a little tense

Did I tell what happened the time I found a wooden shoe in the toilet?

What happens when you put eggs on the shopping list?

They roll off

Did I ever tell you about the time Granny couldn't pay her water bill?

I sent her a Get Well Soon card

WHAT DID THE SNAIL RIDING ON THE TURTLE'S BACK SAY?

Wheeeee!

How does a farmer keep track of his cattle?

A horse walks into a bar. The bartender says, "Why the long face?"

What do you call a bee that can't make up its mind?

A May-bee

What did the two pieces of bread say on their wedding day?

It was loaf at first sight

Why didn't the toilet paper make it across the road?

How do you fix a broken pumpkin?

With a pumpkin patch

Why is the mushroom always invited to parties?

He's a fungi

WHAT DID THE FULL GLASS SAY TO THE EMPTY GLASS?

You look drunk

Why did the skeleton burp?

Because it didn't have the guts to fart

CHAPTER
THREE

REALLY EMBARRASSING DAD JOKES

"By the time a man realizes that maybe his father was right, he usually has a son who thinks he's wrong."

Charles Wadsworth

What do you call a factory that makes okay chairs?

A sat-isfactory

A skeleton walks into a bar and says, "Hey, bartender. I'll have one beer and a mop."

WHERE DO BOATS GO WHEN THEY'RE SICK?

To the boat dock

What do you call it when a snowman throws a tantrum?

What do you call a girl in the middle of a tennis court?

Annette

WHAT KIND OF SANDALS DO FROGS WEAR?

What is a calendar's favourite food?

Dates

My three favourite things are eating my family and not using commas.

HOW DO YOU MAKE HOLY WATER?

You boil the hell out of it

What do you call a bull before he grows his horns?

What do clouds wear when they want to look elegant?

WHY CAN YOU NEVER BURN A HAWAIIAN PIZZA?

What's the leading cause of dry skin?

Towels

If you're American when you go into the toilet, and you're American when you come out, what are you while you're in there?

Which knight invented King Arthur's Round Table?

Sir Cumference

WHAT DO YOU GET WHEN YOU CROSS A SNOWMAN WITH A VAMPIRE?

What do you call a huge pile of cats?

A meow-ntain!

WHERE DO PENCILS COME FROM?

What falls down but never needs a bandage?

The rain

WHAT MONTH IS THE SHORTEST OF THE YEAR?

May – it only has three letters

WHAT DO YOU CALL A DOG WITH NO LEGS?

You can call him whatever you want, he's still not coming

Q: "Dad, can you put my shoes on?"

A: "No, I don't think they'll fit me."

Wanna hear a joke about a pizza?

Never mind, it's too cheesy

Whatever happened to the man who was addicted to the hokey pokey?

HOW DOES PASTA ENTER A HOUSE?

Gnocchi

What's the opposite of a hot dog?

A chili dog

WHAT AWARD DOES A DENTIST GET FOR BEING THE BEST?

A little plaque

What do you call a fish that can breakdance?

CHAPTER
FOUR

VINTAGE DAD JOKES

"Raising kids is part joy...
and part guerrilla warfare."
Ed Asner

WHAT DID THE VET SAY TO THE CAT?

How are you feline?

Where do math teachers go on vacation?

What does garlic do when it gets hot?

It takes its cloves off

What do kids play when they have nothing else to do?

WHAT DID THE TREE SAY WHEN SPRING FINALLY ARRIVED?

What a re-leaf

Did you hear about the bossy man at the bar?

WHAT DO YOU CALL A MAN WEARING A RUG ON HIS HEAD?

Matt

How do you tell
the difference
between a bull
and a cow?

What do you call people who really like tractors?

Protractors!

Why can't a nose be 12 inches long?

Did you hear about the dad who invented the knock-knock joke?

He won the Nobel Prize

Why did the dad sell his vacuum cleaner?

How do you make a water bed bouncier?

Add spring water

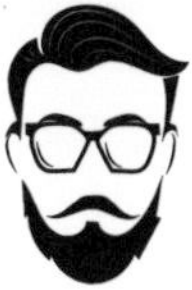

WHY DID THE COFFEE CALL THE POLICE?

It got mugged

How do you get an astronaut's baby to sleep?

Rocket

Why did the nose get angry at the finger?

What kind of car does a sheep like to drive?

A Lamborghini

How do you talk to a giant?

WHAT'S A SEA MONSTER'S FAVOURITE LUNCH?

Fish and ships

What do you call a line of men waiting to get haircuts?

What vegetable is cool, but not that cool?

Radish

Why did the dinosaur cross the road?

WANNA HEAR A JOKE ABOUT PAPER?

Never mind. It's tearable!

Sometimes I tuck my knees into my chest and lean forward.

What goes down but doesn't come up?

A yo

What do you call a lazy baby kangaroo?

A pouch potato!

WHAT KIND OF SHOES DO NINJAS WEAR?

Sneakers!

What do clouds wear?

CHAPTER
FIVE

SUPER SILLY DAD JOKES

"If you're not yelling at your kids,
you aren't spending enough time
with them."
Mark Ruffalo

What do you call a bear with no teeth?

A gummy bear

What kind of music scares balloons?

WHY ARE FISH SO SMART?

Because they swim in schools

Have you heard the joke about the bed?

No? That's because it hasn't been made yet

What's the difference between Prince William and a tennis ball?

One is heir to the throne and one is thrown in the air

What do you get when you combine a rhetorical question and a dad joke?

What kind of cat likes living in water?

An octo-puss

WHY SHOULD YOU NEVER GO TO WAR WITH AN OCTOPUS?

It's well-armed

What's the difference between a well-dressed man on a unicycle and a poorly dressed man on a bike?

Attire!

HOW DOES MOSES MAKE HIS TEA?

WHAT'S GREEN AND SHAKES ITS HIPS?

Elvis Parsley

How do young bees get to school?

WHY DO GHOSTS LOVE ELEVATORS?

Because they lift their spirits

How do prisoners communicate with one another?

Cell phones

143

Why was the picture angry it went to jail?

Because it was framed!

WHY CAN'T A LEOPARD HIDE?

Because he's always spotted

What did the earthquake say when it was finished?

Sorry, my fault!

What's black and white and goes around and around?

Why don't eggs tell jokes?

They'd crack each other up

What do you do when you see a spaceman?

How do you think the unthinkable?

With an ithberg!

How do you catch a bra?

With a booby trap

How many ears do space aliens have?

Three: the left ear, right ear and the final front ear

What do hillbillies drink from?

3.14 PER CENT OF SAILORS ARE *PI-RATES.*

What do you get when you cross a polar bear with a seal?

If athletes get athlete's foot, what do rocket scientists get?

Missile toe

WHY WAS HARRY POTTER'S COMPUTER MAGICAL?

CHAPTER
SIX

THE BEST OF THE WORST DAD JOKES

"Whenever one of my children
says, 'Goodnight, Daddy,'
I always think to myself,
'You don't mean that.'"
Jim Gaffigan

Did the hear about the ice cream truck accident?

It crashed on a rocky road!

HOW CAN YOU TELL THE DIFFERENCE BETWEEN A DOG AND A TREE?

What's brown and sticky?

A stick

What's a scarecrow's favourite fruit?

What does a painter do when he gets cold?

Puts on another coat

What do you call recently married spiders?

Newly-webs

Why do birds fly south in winter?

Because it's too far to walk

What do you call 26 letters that went for a swim?

HOW DO YOU WEIGH YOUR TEENAGE SISTER?

In Instagrams

What invention allows us to see through walls?

What did the sock say to the smelly foot?

Shoe!

Where do pirates buy hooks?

What has four wheels and flies?

A bin man's truck

What do Santa's elves learn at school?

What does a baby computer call his father?

Data

What kinds of pictures do hermit crabs take?

What kind of tea is the hardest to swallow?

Reality

What do you call someone who points out the obvious?

What did the fish say when it swam into the wall?

Dam!

WHAT DO YOU CALL A CAVEMAN THAT WANDERS AROUND AIMLESSLY?

A meander-thal!

WHY DO MELONS HAVE WEDDINGS?

Because they cantaloupe

Did you hear about the dad who stayed up all night wondering where the sun went?

What did the man say to the surgeon after a brain transplant?

I've changed my mind

What's blue and smells like red paint?

What do you call a horse that doesn't have a home?

Unstable

WHAT DID THE RIGHT EYE SAY TO THE LEFT EYE?

Why did the farmer plough his field with a steamroller?

He was trying to grow mashed potatoes

What's green, green, green?

What did the hat say to the other hat?

You go on ahead

How much do roofs cost?

Nothing. They're on the house!

What do you call a cold parrot?

A brrr-d

What's worse than finding a worm in your apple?

Why did the orange stop halfway across the road?

It ran out of juice